T0005600

MAMAS
and
BABIES

For Jackie Bear.

—CM

RISE × Penguin Workshop
An imprint of Penguin Random House LLC, New York

First published in the United States of America by Rise × Penguin Workshop,
an imprint of Penguin Random House LLC, New York, 2024

Copyright © 2024 by Christie Matheson

Penguin supports copyright. Copyright fuels creativity, encourages diverse voices, promotes free speech, and creates a vibrant culture. Thank you for buying an authorized edition of this book and for complying with copyright laws by not reproducing, scanning, or distributing any part of it in any form without permission. You are supporting writers and allowing Penguin to continue to publish books for every reader.

PENGUIN is a registered trademark and PENGUIN WORKSHOP is a trademark of Penguin Books Ltd.
The W and RISE Balloon colophons are registered trademarks of Penguin Random House LLC.

Visit us online at penguinrandomhouse.com.

Library of Congress Cataloging-in-Publication Data is available.

Manufactured in China

ISBN 9780593659281   10 9 8 7 6 5 4 3 2 1 HH

The text is set in Ashley Script MT Std and Maltese.
The art was painted using watercolor on paper.

Edited by Nicole Fox
Designed by Maria Elias

MAMAS
and
BABIES

BY CHRISTIE MATHESON

RISE

NEW YORK

"A mother's love for her child
is like nothing else in the world."
—Agatha Christie

FROM THE MOMENT THEY WAKE,

polar bear cubs spend as much time as they can with their mama. They play and slide with her, and climb on her for piggyback rides through the snow.

WHEN A JOEY IS BORN,

he's only the size of a jelly bean!

So he stays nuzzled inside mama

kangaroo's cozy pouch for six months,

drinking her milk to help him

grow strong.

MAMA PENGUIN GOES ON

a long, brave journey to the ocean to find food for her chick. When she returns, she fills her baby's hungry belly with food from her own mouth.

A NEWBORN FAWN'S

little legs are very wobbly!

But with mama deer's gentle help,

she quickly learns to stand

and take steps all by herself.

MAMA SWAN TEACHES HER

cygnets to swim soon after they are born.

When they get tired and need a break,

the cygnets climb up onto their mama's

back to rest in her soft, warm feathers.

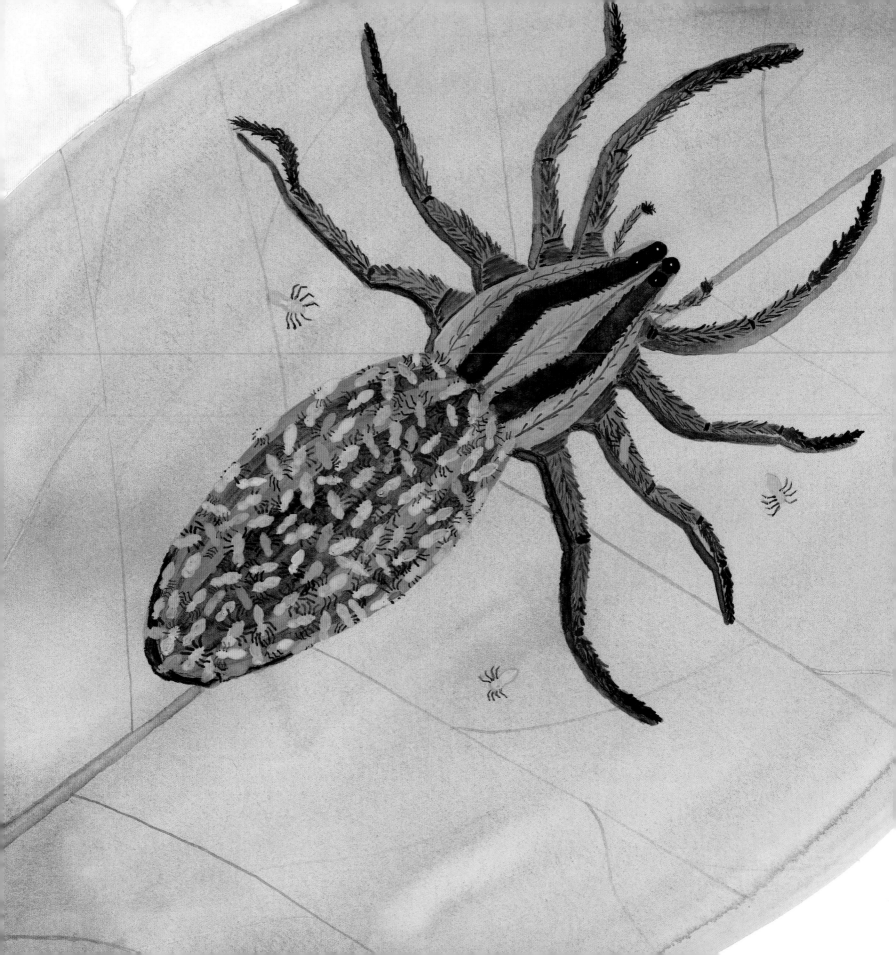

AFTER HUNDREDS OF HER

spiderlings hatch, mama wolf spider

carries them all on her back, wanting

to keep them close and safe as she goes

through her day.

MAMA ALLIGATOR PROTECTS

her hatchlings by gently carrying them inside of her mouth. She keeps them tucked in safely behind her sharp teeth as she takes them to the water to swim.

MAMA HUMPBACK WHALE WHiSPERS

softly to her calf in the water, so he feels safe knowing

she is always nearby. Her calf whispers back,

staying quiet so no one else can hear.

WHEN iT'S BATH TiME,

mama elephant uses her long

trunk to spray and scrub her

calf clean, and to wrap her in

giant hugs!

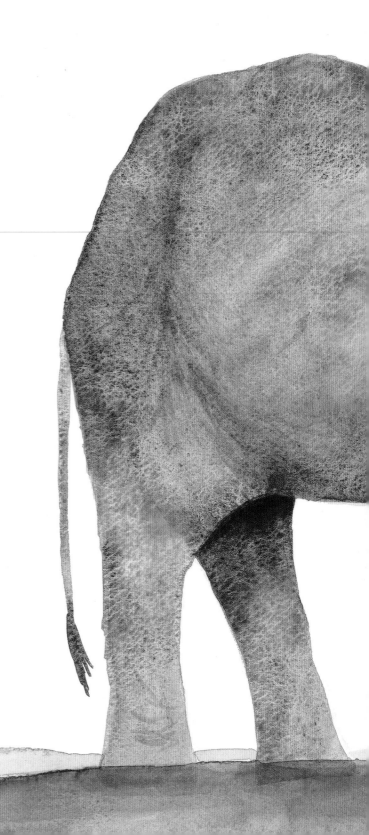

MAMA CHEETAH BATHES HER

cubs daily with lots of wet kisses. And her cubs give her plenty of licks right back!

A GiRAFFE CALF NEEDS

lots of sleep, so mama stays awake

through the night to watch for

danger and keep him safe

while he rests.

BABY ORANGUTAN LOVES TO

hold his mama's strong hand—while

they swing through the treetops, as they

walk through the forest, and when they

snuggle in together for bedtime.

MAMA GRIZZLY BEAR AND HER CUBS

spend the winter months cuddling inside of

their den, keeping each other warm and safe

as they sleep together.

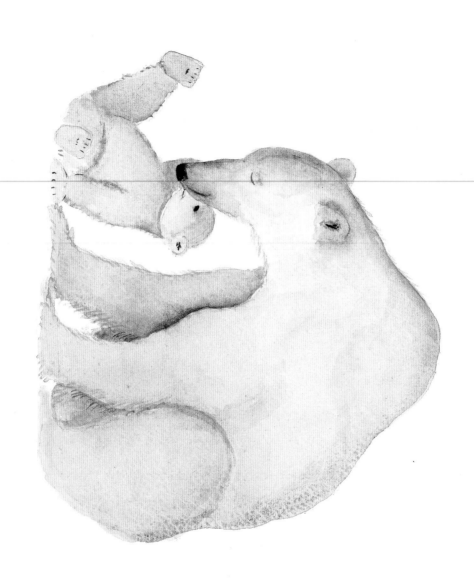